I've got questions

Do Baby Bears Have Mommies?

written by Crystal Bowman and Teri McKinley | illustrated by Ailie Busby

TYNDALE KIDS

Tyndale House Publishers, Inc.
Carol Stream, IL

Visit Tyndale's website for kids at www.tyndale.com/kids.

Library of Congress Cataloging-in-Publication Data
Names: Bowman, Crystal, author.
Title: Do baby bears have mommies? / written by Crystal Bowman and Teri
   McKinley.
Description: Carol Stream, IL : Tyndale House Publishers, Inc., 2017. |
   Series: I've got questions
Identifiers: LCCN 2016015555 | ISBN 9781496417404 (hc)
Subjects: LCSH: Animals--Religious aspects--Christianity--Juvenile
   literature. | Animals--Juvenile literature.
Classification: LCC BT746 .B69 2017 | DDC 261.8/8--dc23 LC record available at https://lccn.loc.gov/2016015555

Printed in China

23	22	21	20	19	18	17
7	6	5	4	3	2	1

To Karen D. V.—
my go-to gal.
—C. B.

To Conner West—
May your life be filled with adventure!
—T. M.

All the animals of the forest are mine,
and I own the cattle on a thousand hills.
I know every bird on the mountains,
and all the animals of the field are mine.

Psalm 50:10-11

Kids have lots of questions!
Do you have questions too—
of bugs and bears and elephants
and monkeys at the zoo?

2

God made your mind amazing.
There's so much you can know.
Learning is a lot of fun.
Get ready, set—let's go!

3

Do baby bears have mommies
that give them food to eat?
And when it's cold and snowy,
do cubs get chilly feet?

Mommy bears feed
baby cubs
with berries, nuts,
or bugs.
They snuggle closely
in their dens
with warm and
furry hugs.

4

5

Can ladybugs be girls or boys?
It seems so strange to me
that something called a ladybug
could be a she or he.

Ladybugs are
    boys and girls—
they almost look
    the same.
The smaller ladybugs are boys,
but both bugs share the name.

When elephants get sleepy,
do they lay their giant heads
on big, white, fluffy pillows
while dreaming in their beds?

Elephants don't sleep for long,
because it hurts their bones.
They don't have big,
    white pillows;
they sleep on dirt and stones.

8

9

How do earthworms
dig in dirt
and move across the ground?
Earthworms don't have
hands or feet
to help them crawl around.

Worms have little bristles
and muscles that are strong.
They stretch their bodies
back and forth;
that's how they
move along.

10

11

Why are eagles' wings so long—
is that what helps them fly?
Do they flap their wings a lot
while soaring through the sky?

Eagles flap their
wings to fly,
but sometimes
they can glide.
When God sends gusty
paths of wind,
they swoop in
for a ride.

12

13

Do monkeys like bananas?
Is that their favorite treat?
And when they eat their dinner,
do they use their hairy feet?

Monkeys eat their
    vegetables.
They like bananas, too.
They use their hands
    or feet to eat—
that's just what
    monkeys do.

14

15

Kangaroos just make me laugh.
Their pouches look so funny!
Tell me what they keep in there—
some jelly beans or money?

A mama kangaroo's
big pouch
is for her baby 'roo.
She keeps her joey
safe and warm
and feeds him in
there too.

16

Why are skunks so stinky?
I can smell them in the air.
Do they need to brush their teeth
or wash their dirty hair?

It's not their teeth or dirty hair
that makes skunks smell that way.
When they sense danger coming,
they lift their tails and spray.

18

19

I like to hear the cows say moo
while eating in the sun.
Are they talking to their babies?
Are they mooing just for fun?

A mama cow moos loudly
when her babies
wander off.
But when her calves are
by her side,
her moo is very soft.

Goo! Moo!

Do mice have little houses
that they can sneak inside?
Or do they live in forests,
where they can run and hide?

Mice build homes in grassy fields
or snuggle in the hay.
They even burrow underground
if it's a chilly day.

22

Giraffes have long and skinny necks
that hold their heads up high.
Why are they so long and tall?
They almost touch the sky!

Giraffes eat yummy, crispy
leaves
that grow up high on trees.
Their long necks help them
reach their food
to eat it with great ease.

25

Why do ducks have funny feet
and feathers on their backs?
Why do they swim all around
and make those noisy quacks?

Ducks have feet that help
    them swim.
Their feathers keep them dry.
Quacking is the way they talk.
It's how a duck says hi!

26

God made all the animals,
and each one is unique.
He made the worms and bugs
that crawl
and furry mice that squeak.

28

He made amazing creatures
on land and in the air.
And every creature he has made
is always in his care.

29

More books by

Crystal Bowman and Teri McKinley

My Mama & Me
Rhyming Devotions for You and Your Child
ISBN 978-1-4143-7973-9

M is for Manger
written by Crystal Bowman & Teri McKinley
pictures by Claire Keay
ISBN 978-1-4964-2004-6

THE ONE YEAR
DEVOTIONS for Preschoolers
Illustrated by Elena Kucharik
Little Blessings
ISBN 978-0-8423-8940-2

I've got questions
Do Baby Bears Have Mommies?
written by Crystal Bowman and Teri McKinley | illustrated by Ailie Busby
ISBN 978-1-4964-1740-4

I've got questions
Does God Take Naps?
written by Crystal Bowman and Teri McKinley | illustrated by Ailie Busby
ISBN 978-1-4964-1741-1

Purchase these books online or at your favorite retailer.

CP1236